Between Two Hemispheres

Also by Adrian Rogers and published by Ginninderra Press
The Sun Behind the Sun
Seasons, Situations & Symbols (Pocket Poets)

Adrian Rogers

Between Two Hemispheres

Between Two Hemispheres
ISBN 978 1 74027 921 5
Copyright © text Adrian Rogers 2015
Cover images: gum leaves © robynmac – fotolia.com
shamrock leaves © naddya – fotolia.com

First published 2015 by
GINNINDERRA PRESS
PO Box 3461 Port Adelaide SA 5015
www.ginninderrapress.com.au

Contents

Introduction	7
The Migration Myth	7
Wild Geese Flying South	9
One South – A Dreaming	11
The Mystery of the Barrage	13
River Mouth Reflections	15
Oscar W	18
Six Mount Crawford War Dances…	20
Two North – The Irish Connection	29
Innisfree Idealised	31
Supplicating Arms	32
Western Winter Land and Seascape	33
St Patrick's Vision	34
West of Ireland Patchwork Quilt	36
Croagh Patrick	37
Connemara	38
Three South – Gnostic Vision	41
The Bubble of Time	43
The Gnostic's Lonely Choices	44
Hermetic Journey	46
To the One Cryptic Self	48
Mirror of Renunciation	50
Letting Go	51
Four North – Through the Connemara Landscape…	53
1 Painting the Backdrop	55
2 Place Defines Vision	57
3 Music Plays Its Part	58
4 The Questers Set Sail	59
5 Towards Enlightenment…	61
6 A Return to Something	62

7 A Temporary Resting Place	63
8 Some Are Never Satisfied	64
9 The Never Ending Seekers	65
10 The Quest Remains Unfinished	66

Five South – Looking Out and About	67
Two From New Papua Guinea	69
Tanami	71
Line of Defence	73
The Edge	74
Winter	80
Wooden Boat Man	81
Afterglow	83

Six Between Two Hemispheres	85
Wild Geese	87
On the Ebb	89
Empty Nest	90
Heart and Head	91
Between Two Hemispheres	92

Introduction

The Migration Myth

Wild Geese Flying South

A wind toss
flings a bell toll
backwards and forwards
as wild geese fly south
beyond assonance
and dissonance

two hemispheres call
across an age's dreaming
as wings ride the wind
to horizons at nightfall
vanishing
their lure detached
from scheming
at the homing touchdown,
shards of hope and meaning
sharp-edged ambitions
tall or small
looking sunwards
'Eyes wide shut!'

The oratory is empty
holy well, turf fire,
sea echoing shell
ancestral memory sublimated
by the heart's desire
because, 'The Heart has its reasons'

a long
interrupted echo wave
may call them back
from heat, dust,

a red-centre's dazzle
of sun-glare mirages,
white coasts, tall forests,
strange seasons
yet not as at their going,
for they have known
less travelled ways
between two hemispheres.

One

South – A Dreaming

The Mystery of the Barrage

Rain, cloud and mist
sweep the barrage
gull cries a punctuating commentary
river island and mainland
with outreaching
concrete and iron arm
linked across wind-ruffled space.

Green reeds line the shallows
like frilled cuffs on a sleeve
a gaggle of geese intersperse the shadow loom
terns soar and swoop in the inter-space
fresh and saltwater an interrupted mingling.

Walk over water
where ongoing volumes
of long river distances
replete with urban and rural memories
are held back
where fresh meets salt
from a wide-skied estuarine
limitlessly halfway world
beyond the barrage
seabirds, dunes,
a tuned chorus of wind in grass,
the only constant
a distant surf roar,
a mystery
of historical freshwater miles
anticipating
that goal of all flowings

raindrop, dewdrop, creek and river
barred from end and beginning
the sea.

River Mouth Reflections

1

Light and clouds sky-pattern dance over the river mouth
the surf is a constant of white foam wings

a kaleidoscopic, intermingling shrub and grass green subtlety
a blue-grey shimmering between the land's arms
coming and going sun shafts uniting
in bird flight flock clusters and scatterings

swept wind songs earth coloured
on water and across wide spaces blending
are musical asymmetry
echo-haunted sedges, wave-patterned
light's descent reflected back
elusive
a rhythmic interchange
between above and below.

2

Walk over river ways
between outstretching sand fingers

a sharp intermittent wind
rain gusts, an alternating
cloud/mist fantasia

the line dancers
at a fresh and salt water meeting
mingle and parade across the last barrage.

3

Magic of wildness
fleeting light and shadow
over wind bitten grasses
crouching shrubs
and water running
under wide-scanning cloud and blue sky

this, the enchanted moment
is a time out of time.

4

Across free flowing water channels
and wet sand bars
under white flying streamers
a muffled surf roar beyond the river mouth
is an always breaking thunder

a running shadow
flits wildly across wide
cloud-flecked skies
and pale cream dunes
unable to escape
the grip of wiry weathered grasses
resounding, in the giving back of light.

5

Rain showers the mood changers
brush carelessly bleached grasses
samphire flats and bushes cringing
against a singing wind's whip

a high-voice enchantment
pierced randomly by bird calls
is abandonment to rise and fall
dashed by sun-catching wings.

6

Sandpiper at the water's edge
go not beyond the shallows
call back the summer's
light and water interplay
its orchestration of the wave rush
and the wind,
for with your northward passing
will the autumn bring
thinned-out light, shorter days
or voices merely drifting
across dreamscapes of memory.

Oscar W

A river boat's dreaming

The slap
of water on wood
a steamboat's hull
paddles inert
engine idle
tourists drifting about the decks
or peering through wheelhouse glass
hands gripping
the helm's skeletal metal curve
triggers dream/self-projections
into river-borne adventures
still reverberant
when they stare into the galley
where stove-piled wood
purveys illusions
of purposeful busyness
rough and ready meals
in different river ports
yet not beyond the slap
of water on wood
a steamboat moored
to her present
inarticulate destiny.

Does she remember the past
the smother and clatter
machinery on wooden wharves
voices, heat, dust and sweat,
loading, unloading
bales, sacks, boxes, packages,
the displacement of ballast?

Was this more
than water on wood
the then present destiny
of a steamboat's hull?

Was it more than today?

Six Mount Crawford War Dances Between Plantation and Bush

1 Green Saraband

A dark green gloom
of pines processional
in drooping sarabande
unfold across
declining slopes
towards a road
as if to smother
the heedless crawl
of cars like shining beetles
unless ruffled reservoir water
tracked by bright pale
slanting light
off the road's far side
is preferable
to a green cloud overwhelming.

2 The Witnesses

The pines halted
expose beside
a pale brown
curving dirt track
a weather-beaten chapel's
soberly grey
broken-walled silence
under lowering skies
deepening
a green tide's held back
resentful sweep
against significantly
eroded masonry
and tilting tombstones
silent witness
in worn inscriptions.

3 The Rusting Gate

Sprawling bush
has stemmed
an implacably shadowed green wave,
assembling to hold
one side of this track
against the pines.

A rusting gate
at a by-path's end
half smothered
by bleached skeletal mazes
of trunks and branches
elusively clad
in grey/green
breeze ruffled shades
awaits a challenge
to an official sign
unofficially askew
forbidding trespass.

4 The Path

Beyond the gate
a winding path
is intruded upon,
over-crossed by
tangled branches
networked
in green to silver
olive-hinting shrouds
of soft-voiced leaves
as footsteps crunch
brittle bark twigs
and dry foliage
wakening subtle
sharp scents
of bushland incense,
until a shot sharp
wood snap interjecting
a magpie call is…
what?

5 I am Shadow

The retreat was a rout.

A division of pines
outflanked, outfought,
defeated the bush
so everywhere
and nowhere
I am shadow no substance
in a shadow-cast
whispering coniferous loom
constrained by
black soberly straight
parading trunks
yet the bush
time displaced
not locatable
is present unseen
except inwardly
silenced
by correctness
its unformalised inner order
replaced
by a structurally functional
'trooping the colour'
from green to black.

Those pines
clothed across sloping boughs
in spaced green
hanging clusters
overshadowing
a brown carpet's
time-expired needles
are standing to attention
for the salute.

6 The Archer at the Gates

After my novel *The Gates of Sunset*

Silence
is a circular space,
riotous bush awestruck
at finding itself restrained
by a shallowly concave openness
short grass clad,
significantly potent
with intrusive
yet arrested growth
revealing
a sky-bounded
far-side emptiness
framed
by two dark
shadow-casting pillars
west facing.

Will the Archer
in the Gates
send an arrow
from that infinite edge
if I step beyond pine and bush?

Will artifice and nature
jostle as before
interrupted by vineyards
or will
the Gates of Sunset
be a gateway
to a water-wide world's
light, shadow,
myth and legend
come alive
in arrow flight
and spear cast?

Two

North – The Irish Connection

Innisfree Idealised

Lough Gill, Co. Sligo

From the road above the loch
Innisfree
scrub covered green
edged brown
red autumn tinted
not particularly distinguished
seen distantly
against grey water/bright sheen
looks lonely
as if being uninhabited
reflected anticlimax
after anticipation.

One wonders why Yeats clothed it
in so spellbindingly
'dropping slow' a dream
of exile
unless he saw
behind appearances
a darkness rising
from watery depths
turn soundlessly
to pale serpentine wisps
dancing
the 'Fiddler of Dooney's signature tune
echoing across
a shadowed shimmering
from his pointed finger rock.

Supplicating Arms

Connemara

These woods do not like
cold salt Atlantic breath
the wailing persistence
of prevailing winds
shivering
rustling withered brown leaves
against gales,
their branches
are supplicating arms
bending away from seaborne fury
like victims
shielding themselves from assault.

Protecting trunks
and roots gripping
nutrient-starved earth
let winter's forces
flanked by
capriciously violent equinoxes
deflect them
like politicians
responding to the vagaries
of public opinion.

Why, beyond hope of change
do stunted trees endure
elements
predictable only
in their unpredictability?

Western Winter Land and Seascape

Co. Mayo

A bay's far-flung
south-west curve
and winter pale sands
offset
overlooking mountain peaks
grey to deep purple
under dark
cloud-weighted skies

seafront hotels and shops
seem out of place
clinging
to a last solid ledge
above advancing waves
rank on rank
in line abreast
topped whitely
with pennants of flying foam.

The tide's flood
inexorable as its ebb
interacts with drooping overcast
shades-of-green patterned land
and off-white sand
on beaches tourist-empty

a shell's crunch underfoot
interrupts
the wind's unsteady moan,
sea, sky, and earth
can be themselves again.

St Patrick's Vision

A voice called
from the wood of Focluth
where tangled oak scrub
almost meets
the western sea's wild weathered shore
inland
the trees stood taller
but almost leaf-stripped
by relentless autumn winds.

'Come over and help us, holy boy,'
the speaker said…

nothing heard or seen
is recalled
beyond untamed wood, voice,
and beckoning hand.

I was enslaved
by others of his kind
until I fled
from winter gales and snuffling pigs;
how could I willingly return
to memories of a barbarous servitude?

Yet refusal's deafness
would be tantamount
to turning back
from true enlightenment
into the dark.

Could I decline to shine for them
the light which since that bitter time
has lit my days?

West of Ireland Patchwork Quilt

Above Glencar, Co. Sligo

The land, a patchwork quilt
stone-bordered emerald squares
and dark-wooded interjections
soft rain-rinsed
or shower-swept
under a seamless gloom
awaits
almost forgotten
sun-lightening interludes
from grey dulled
to pearly luminosity
making the earth
exhale hazes
scarcely veiling
fey and timeless things

flashing silver
interpenetrating air and light
indirectly
half perceived peripherally
momentary capturers
of mind, heart and small realities
uncomprehending
true otherness,
yet attuned to beauty
terror, mystery
beyond the world's end
and enchantment
challenging the lure
of ordinariness.

Croagh Patrick

A work in progress

A climber's life path
skyward emerges sequentially
above sprawling
stone-walled fields
grey/tumbled boulder-strewn
abruptly green
from lowland haze
where journeys are more
than destinations
and a distant sunburst chime
echoing a rhyme
is a bell tolled for pilgrim generations,
beyond mist veils
towards the light break
on an almost pyramidal peak
actualising beyond cloud sweeps
a seaward vista's
emerald sparking islands
out-flung onto blue,
a work in progress
beyond sunburst chime
rhyme
and a bell tolled for pilgrim generations.

Connemara

A train journey through time, looking back to 1964

A glass divided landscape
slips past the dining car
rounded mountains hazed-over mauve
shaped 'Celtic Twilight' insinuations,
old weathered, 'Lordly' magic cut
by rolling metal discords
as emigrated
timelessly sheep-scattered valleys
materialise
in reflection.

Reality like a ship's wake
is reflected in limewashed
rain-blue stained cottages
red fuchsia splashed
tantalising peripheral vision.

A sun shaft
pathways stripped dark
a turf bog, and brown stacks loom
against silver-low clouds
as a pannier-laden donkey
steps tiredly
into pearl-iridescent afternoon
but the old, tradition-trapped
colour-recollected life bubble
vanishes
pricked out by jack hammers
and computers, unanswered
by reverberations irritating coffee cups
as postcard scenery
glides unstoppably
like change
beyond the point of no return.

Three

South – Gnostic Vision

The Bubble of Time

Bursting
the bubble of time
for freedom
undegenerated
in space
dreams, climbing
the silver cord ladder
break
into light
multitudinous forms
colours
infinite perceptions
beyond sharp
clear-cut horizons.

The body, sleep-bound
reveals imperfections
unflatteringly
yet nothing temporal matters
on spiritual
spatial
multilevel soul flight.

Only jarring
spirit/body
imperfectly aligned returns
for the long march
shatter
the vase of dreams,
spilling its contents
into wakefulness.

The Gnostic's Lonely Choices

They started with one
then on to gnosis
experienced beyond
the information super-highway
through space-time
continua of chant
largo stepped-out ceremonial's
measured pace
in sharp response
to incense clouds
across a pendulum-like arc,
while smoke reacted
and interacted
with naked flame
and revelatory chordal vibrations
variously sublimated
blended, more
than sums of parts
layered like tree rings
in rejection, of
religious informality
packaged
in linguistic journalese
dumbed-down
to chattering manners.

To such the Gnostic would
and will not genuflect
but turned
and turns instead
to ritually engendered awe
a path to silence
priesthood and poetry
like the gravitas
of water darkening
under hanging cliffs
and alone
to the alone
journeyed
and journeys inflexibly
on, and on.

Hermetic Journey

A cell's stonewalled
confined disquiet
is a world uncontainable
beyond the monastic vegetable patch.

Vision
against lamplight
in awful
speaking silence
creates
with rain-scattered windows
and doors undercut
by bone-punishing draughts
a stretched
page wandering
paper-thin concentration
on the square.

Crowded images
are night walkers
of terrible insubstantiality
and dark terror's
infinitely fire-tongued challenge.

To tip the balance
for return
along the sun path
freed, from toss
and dice throw
the gnostic seer
actualises
two sides of the same coin
between
the compass points.

To the One Cryptic Self

When a vessel wind-driven
cuts loose, sail billowing
against overmastering blue
and light is perceived
as an eye blink
in the spectrum
of eternity,
timelessness
is focused into time
in a real irradiation
from within
not beyond the One Self
neither above
nor below
but as gnosis apprehended
against illusions
of a vanishing horizon.

This we possess
through cycles of our time
at the displacement
of an age
when minds meet
for interchange
in the cusp of light
with the resonance
of one note
unheard but echoing
along stone-hard roads

because we travel
to the shorelines
of the everlasting seas
and that moment
of eternal embarkation
when the sail
cuts the sky roof…

much more
than phantoms of transition
when All
are One.

Mirror of Renunciation

Edged out sensuality
marginalised
by cloistered stone
haunts…
black diamonds, squares,
turns notes clustered
and alone
on yellowed music pages,
and evening veiled
in sounded memories
earthed
soaring
not quite freely
androgynised
beyond his stability.

Only cold floor
arched vault
and rainbow-faceted window
give back
his stolen dreams.

Letting Go

In memoriam

Leave it
light, shadow, cold
leaden dulled short days
and deceptive winter mildness.

It is no longer yours
dawn chorus
a ripple-running curlew call
sharp wind off the sea
hinting wildness.

Leave it
as it left you
the fading footfall
like a lengthening evening
subsiding into stillness.

Leave remembered moments
when the road outside was quiet
footstep and car free
and silence was a fullness.

Leave it
by an open window
with the sun take flight
into the greater
from a lesser light
dark, or half-lit shadow things
stress, hurry,
and untamed thoughts
unravelling into calmness.

Leave the tree fallen
earth unturned
the fire unlit
quiet unbroken,
for you bereft
of material illusion
have left the veil of sense
and journeyed far beyond
the darkness.

Four

North – Through the Connemara Landscape in Ten Poems

1 Painting the Backdrop

A light breeze
stipples the bay's
gold over blue-flecked waters
and a chill breathed sigh
echoes
with subtle resonance
distant Atlantic swells
above cloud-mirrored
panoramic seashore wanderings.

From a low-lying
rock-tumbled
sand-fringed world
I catch insidious scents
burning turf on salt
teasing senses fine-tuned
by memory, mystery
elusively, hauntingly imaged
in that haze enhanced
silvered water-light.

A fluted shower of gull calls
flung down from concave
sky-wide spaces
blend
with free float-falling
skylark songs
over backward-rising
green-brown moorland,

a water, luminescent
and sound kaleidoscope
evoking austere
long-sighted
time-shadowing dreams
beyond the unbreached walls
of realisation.

2 Place Defines Vision

The interface
between sea and sand
remains a chaotic wilderness
of giant dismembered stones
from almost white
to weathered
almost black, green,
weed-streaked
grey barnacle-peppered
and decorated with
black clinging periwinkles
seeking shelter on the undersides

a place of untamed sacredness
impressed by seeping tides
carelessly creating
water-trapping rock pools
eye-like and mirror-clear
where dawn and twilight's
half-awake essences
define hunchbacked
stone-built oratories
weathered
as rock and moor.

3 Music Plays Its Part

A sacred singer
voices the peripatetic eternity
of Gnostic seers
grown from this watery land
of cloud harried light
and grey, eroded stone
folk earth-attached
but called to track the stars
north, east, west,
or south away
through unremembered voyages
because the currents
of enlightenment shift
only to track new courses
beyond west seaward-facing
time-worn and soft-lit
places of past memory.

4 The Questers Set Sail

Clouds, like mortality
cross sheep-speckled hillsides
briefly veiling
silver-pallid light turned gold
by weather-bronzed grass

white wild swans still flock
scattering across
steel-burnished surfaces
light-flashing
reed-fringed
cold loch waters
and weed-slicked inlets
of land-piercing seas
but nothing will detain
those seekers grasping
at the hemlines of eternity
who have hanged material values
upside down.

For them
water-broken and eroded shores
green/brown hills
blue-distanced by the light
and ripple-threading curlew calls
through passing moods of sun and rain,
all…must be surrendered
to the wind-bent sail,
so fiercely loved
but indeterminate borderlands

drop away
as they pass islands risen
like black spurs
through grey-white
surging foam thresh
to find, perhaps
those open-ended refuges
where clouds slide down
a vaulted roof
to meet and merge
with crested seas curled, leaping.

5 Towards Enlightenment…

…till water, light and sky
are magnetised by cloudscapes
into one, beyond the patterning
of thought made solid
by material demands.

So these true voyagers
sail out of time
on song-born
long-inflected cadences
towards the starting point
before that losing
of 'The Robe of Glory'*

behind and past
that long-lost cry
of birthing.

* 'The Robe of Glory' is the title of an ancient Gnostic poem.

6 A Return to Something

A sail aslant against sloping
sea-washed afternoon light
denotes a curragh
familiarly west wind
shoreward-pressed.

A grounding scrape of leather
on wet sliding shingle
scratches the airflow.

The wanderers have returned
from where wild seas
met plunging skies,
and earth sways briefly
under wave-accustomed feet
before they pitch
dun-coloured slouching tents
between rough weathered grass
and beige pale sands.

7 A Temporary Resting Place

A stream passes their camp
flashing silver-gilded
down-running seaward
between turf banks
chocolate brown
as evening stretches itself
unrolling, evolving
long-light carpeting
from thinned-out pearl
to fierce blood-red
dominant
until night's onset
forces the sun's retreat
below a vanishing horizon line.

8 Some Are Never Satisfied

Dawn will resurrect the quest.

They will rise up
in still, cold
clarion-calling light
to fold their tents
cut blackthorn staves
and tramp in hard-worn boots
configuring and supporting
foot-firm marching steps
as restless eyes search lucent
but deceptively changeable horizons
ephemeral
as the dreams they propagate
for ceaseless pilgrims
following esoteric
signpost clues
to where stone crossroads
score a tempting choice
of paths for tired feet
that press on still
towards an unattainable
'Avalon of the Heart'.

9 The Never Ending Seekers

They are beyond the long retreat
of that cloud-shafted
wide curved line.

Light above the sea
is slightly yellowed pearl
below black parallel cloud bars
slashing a west diminishing
water-pale sun
foretelling rain,
with yet another evening's promise
of reflective campsite refuge
made easily
and as easily forgotten.

10 The Quest Remains Unfinished

Their night fire will be
from burning driftwood
the medium for raising
re-imagined towers
spires and walls
of that city haunting them
beyond the last, lost
'Rose Line'
of forbidden liberations
waiting beneath
a rubble-layered vault
to re-enact
the Hanged Man's* renunciations
and break free…

before which
other suns must rise
across wet-moored, silver-dewed
and cold grey seas
shot with white-gold
mist-enshrouded light
because the quest
remains unfinished.

---

* The Hanged Man refers to a card in the tarot deck.

Five

South – Looking Out and About

Two From New Papua Guinea

1 – An Outrigger Between the Islands

Two jewel-green
evening-caressed islands
lie still

a breath-slight breeze
flecks the water
waiting to be touched
by a sun burning red
below clouds striated black
a ghost-silent
white-sailed outrigger glides
between light, shadow,
and a sunset
about to fire the sea.

2 – The Spear Fisherman

Balanced
between sky and sea
on a surface-breaking rock
he stands
blackly still
spear poised
oblivious
to acutely angled
vermillion-splendid light
intent
on moving shadows,
he must time
the eye-blink speed
of his cast
with timeless perfection.

Tanami

The desert archetype

Sand, scrub, and a grey road
ribbon-like across
almost blue to understated
olive greens
is shaded to yellow blurred edges
unobtrusively
staining austerely flat
vaguely horizon-less terrains
where landscape subtleties
are tangibly underscored
by foot-sensed
beige to dull pink
soft-textured sand.

Agnostic Tanami's
reticent response
to heatburn
unpredictable rain
and root-splitting drought
proclaims a frugal sanctuary
in breath caught, sharp
bush incense,
the tang of sun-seared leaf
intensified
against burnt bitumen
a desert's chastity
disassociating itself
from sacred space violations

of burnished
scarab-like highway cars
and tactless road trains
defying the negation
of its timeless mirage.

Line of Defence

Against a dust storm

Sun banished
the sky is smeared over
dulled ochre-hinting beige

the house broods
across a dried-out garden
in breathless stillness
waiting
its line of defence
a grey/green straggle
of wattles and melaleucas
intertwining
like whispering conspirators.

A dust storm
swoops across the oval
lashing
sprawling defenders
flexing
like arm-waving protestors
against the inevitable

but dust is secreted
under closed doors
around windows
on polished surfaces,

closure being merely
a time of waiting
for the storm's passing

and an infusion of light.

The Edge

A six-poem panorama of misfits and a sandshoe

1 Lone Yachtsman

Southern Ocean Concerto in C Minor

On the margins
an outrider's hull
surfs
just in touch
like sound flight
his favourite Rachmaninov
broadcast echoes
across plane-smooth ocean swells
a Southern Ocean concerto
for one touching the edge
music not more mystical
than foam-topped wave runs
under high-flying clouds.

2 The Tramp

Threadbare
with colours indefinitely bleached
neutralised
into age unwashed
a loaded
plastic bag bent figure
tends
towards makeshift shelter
or hostel.

What eye contacting history
communicates
behind a stereotypical mask?

3 The Beachcomber

He combs for driftwood
salt-hiss
blue fire spark
apt flame
for people of the outgoing tide
on beach-run keels
water-kissed
reading wave lift
and sun-winged gulls
while sandshoes turn
sea-damp wrack
and sails flirt unreliably
with breezes.

4 A Sandshoe

The sea retreats

a sandshoe
weed-shrouded
rests
between high and low
waits
half-filled
wet
for the next tide
discarded
in time out
from running with children
watching sandcastles
growing and going,
kicking a beach ball.

5 The Lone Yachtsman Reflects

It was worth costly
destabilising competition
a loner's long distance
surfing communion
with long-backed rollers
to music
beyond relationship risks
in planetary synchronicity…

and to look out
from the inside
with only radio and life raft
between sensibility
the self
and ultimate release was
to be.

6 Eternal Voyagers?

A conclusion for misfits

Fire burns
above high-tide mark
acrid smoke and seaweed rot
blend, dissolving
residues of achievement
savaging memory
like a knife gutting fish.

On the margins
they have turned back
from illusion to reality
sidelined
by unpublicised integrity.

Contoured waves recall them
until keels return
to the landing beach
today's boats
tomorrow's driftwood
transmuted
into ash on the breeze
unremembered
but not insignificant.

Winter

Winter's bleak warmth wanting
is unhelped
by afternoon pale
neutered light
insipidly anticipating
dormant evenings
drawn close
like tight-fitting garments
of disillusion
and cold absorbent sobriety.

Only electric red heaters
soulless radiators
or hot-air fixtures
generate artificial cheer
in places unillumined
by shadow-silhouetting flame.

Earth beat and pulse
slow, sapless,
songless, unstirred
after seasonal abandonment
waits
for life-nerved fingers
rootwards thrust
serpent fire rising
to branch, tip
and crown
the green-bursting chakra
of another spring.

Wooden Boat Man

His Last Stand

Pit lightweight
fibreglass modernity
against sharp new varnish
contextually inseparable
for the wooden boat man
from sea breath
with wood
its particular roll and pitch
on ocean swells
beyond sun-painted
white-faced shoreward breakers
unmistakeable,
as his sail assumes
prevailing wind's good offices

no engine here
for whipped-up shallows thresh
or wild river mouth
disturbances.

Unguaranteed
against lee shore
cross current treachery
he weather reads
with skill, touches
transient security
through wet-gripped gunwales.

Beyond tidal tyrannies
aligned with long-swooped gliders
the petrel kind
he is himself,
unchained
and nothing to leeward
but sea and sky.

Afterglow

Mind loss
slows to a walk
or less
journeying towards
a beyond-the-horizon
sky-edged light,
provoking perhaps
regret
or otherwise
in the loser
but for others
no blunting
of pain-sharp edges
to ameliorate
observed realities
deny that afterglow
in the eyes.

Can they see light
flickering perhaps
as fire sinking
against age-chilled night,
home fire, almost
at, or beyond
the road's end?

Six

Between Two Hemispheres

Wild Geese

Migrations past and present

Wild geese flighting
in an earlier age
knew nothing like this,
the tyranny of distance conquered
and transformation
if not realisation
of unquiet dreams
with the world shrinking
like a sun-dried fruit,
but some things remain
unchangeable
like the cognisance
of irreversible change
highlighting the pain
of parting, beyond
that last land glimpse
beneath a plane's wing
before clouds block off the past.

No more the freewheeling
discomforting monotony
of long ocean voyage endured,
our wild geese—in the Age's cusp
enjoy or survive
seamless illusions of comfort
in rows, fast moving
security dogged,
pretending to possible returns
while promising

a temporary duration
to permanent change
beyond the dividing glass
of an airport lounge.

They lay down the past
not knowing if a flight
when passed
beyond turning back
will become one day
an ancestral remembrance,
while the wind echoes still
their song.

On the Ebb

Life past fifty
is an ebb tide
taking the driftwood of memory
wherever it will

and to the old strand
of past endeavour
is no returning

but forward
is a drift beyond nostalgia
along overgrown tracks…

hopefully to hard-won Gnosis.

Empty Nest

Migration is an empty nest
a dipped wing
the past a shut-slammed door
a wild goose flying
from the sun
a land/water touchdown
somewhere, yet not where
the heart discloses.

Heart and Head

He left with Ireland at heart
for a new world in the head
unwillingly obliged to part
from the past, yet be not wed
to present loves – 'let the dead
bury their dead.'

Between Two Hemispheres

Between north and south
on either side
of the clockwise
equatorial
anticlockwise turning
exiles gather
remembering
wild geese flighting
towards, or away from
the setting sun.

Has the west failed them?

Will they return
on the wings of morning
after the last post
and reveille
because the dying light
has been reborn?

Has the west failed them?

Where east meets west
wild geese call
summoning the saints
from long slumbers.

Let Patrick speak for his people
on the last day,
that the west fail not
but marry the east
with north and south her bridesmaids
across an age's span…

between two hemispheres.

www.ingramcontent.com/pod-product-compliance
Lightning Source LLC
Chambersburg PA
CBHW062139100526
44589CB00014B/1624